HALF HORSE

Chronicles of a Horse Girl

Table of Contents

"Horse, thou art truly a creature without equal, for
you fly without wings and conquer without sword."
Arabian Proverb

Chapter One

The Obsession

It all started when I was born in the year of the horse,1978.

Horses. When I was growing up, all I could think about or talk about was horses. I was OBSESSED and I spent every spare moment with them. I would ride the school bus to and from school daily every year, staring out the window imagining I was on a horse racing the bus, jumping over all the driveways. I started choreographing this cool freestyle reining pattern while listening to Phil Collins' "In the Heat of the Night" when I was in kindergarten. I drew horses, I dreamed about horses. I didn't care about boys or anything else — the only thing that mattered was horses.

I was a sponge for anything horse-related and I'd retain it all. I made boys pretend to be horses, or I would play horse by myself and imagine I was in a show — either the horse or riding a horse! I was president of the 4-H Horse Knowledge Bowl and Saddle Club. I spent every second possible surrounded by them. If high school had been about horses, I would have been valedictorian.

Many, many breeds and most every discipline. Arabians were ALWAYS my favorite. My specialty was.Western and English pleasure horses. But I have done pretty much it all. I loved to team pen and calf rope; dressage was always a favorite. I loved going to fun shows and just playing games all day too. I loved jumping when I was younger, but in my 30s I got out of the ring and found more fun in cowboy races.

I spent my teens and 20's a hardcore arena baby constantly training and showing. I changed much of my perspective on how my equine career was going to go, so I loosened up as I got older and found more pleasure taking in the scenes of Northern Minnesota with a good four-legged friend out on a trail in my 30s.

From my hips to the tips of my toes, there are no numbers for the amount of times I have been kicked or stepped on. I've been kicked in the chest twice, in the back, and once in the face. Hiding injuries as a kid taught me more than how to be tough — it became lessons in how not to get hurt. These are just some of those stories.

Chapter Two

The Recip

I was working at a very large, very prestigious all-equine veterinary facility formerly referred to as P.E.A., in Whitesboro, TX. One early morning, after we had finished the rounds, I walked out of the hospital barn to smoke a cigarette and I was followed by an intern named Beth and another technician named Melissa.

We had housing across the parking lot straight ahead and 3 large paddocks to the right and then to the left just behind the barn was a small pasture with 8 to 10 pregnant recip mares. Those mares had been put there because they were close to their due dates and some little did we know, should have already been put in the barn. These aren't your backyard foals they were carrying, they were carrying future athletes and top performers worth top dollars. We were among the first to deliver cloned horses, 7 Smart Chic Olena foals hit the ground there and I was a part of that.

Well this morning as we walked out there was a sudden commotion from the pasture with the expecting mares. Dirt was flying and so was the herd and I could see one tiny body being run over by his momma. The herd was in a frenzy over the newborn and it wasn't good.

Grabbing a couple nearby lead ropes we ran out to the pasture. I remember getting to the Grey mare as she was plowing over the top of her foal knocking it to the side totally confused and seeing the herd coming towards us as Melissa ran past us flagging them away from our direction.

Beth and I somehow got a rope around the mare's neck and we got a loop around her nose but it slid right off as she was bolting away. Both Beth and I each had an end of the lead rope. I remember at that point I was pushing myself into Beth and trying to push her into the horse as hard as I could and trying to sit on the rope because we thought we were going to have her nose. It happened so fast we didn't have time to drop the rope or let alone move. I saw us pass the point of the mare's hip with Beth smashed between us. And then the next thing I remember, there was her hoof coming up at me, I knew I wasn't going to stop it but I tried to put my arm down to block it from my face.

I don't remember the contact, thankfully I'm sure. I just know that I had my left shoulder pushed up against Beth's right shoulder, and we were facing the escaping mare when the lights were on...then the lights were off...when I came to I was face down facing the opposite direction and Beth was also laying face down, motionless about 30 or 40 feet away from me.

I thought she was dead, I just knew her proximity would have put her face into the equation for striking distance.

I saw Melissa running right past Beth and I was pointing for her to turn to help Beth as I was scrambling trying to get to my knees so I could crawl to safety before I got trampled. Now as you might have guessed I had the wind knocked out of myself several times at this point of my life and this didn't feel like normal wind getting knocked out. But I was more concerned about Beth. As I was crawling under the fence the guys that worked in the barns had arrived and were on the scene to help take over the rescue.

Fortunately Beth was kicked in the shoulder not the face. My hoody had a perfect muddy hoofprint left directly on my right lower rib. Melissa kept insisting that I go to the emergency room and while I was having a difficult time breathing, I wasn't sure I was broken. So I took a minute and wanted to smoke a cigarette. I figured if I could smoke I didn't break anything. As I tried to smoke my cigarette she said "Amy I know you felt it, but you didn't see it and you didn't *hear* it."

I thought about it for a second and figured maybe if there was a sound maybe she could be right. So I called my ex to let him know and we headed to the ER. Once we got there they wanted to put me in a wheelchair and neck brace and I wouldn't let them!! After some X-rays I was left only with a massive contusion to my chest. I declined the pain injection (I regretted it later) and was on my way. I was given a day off from work and the mare and foal were brought into the barn, given a stall and technicians were banned from going in with her......except for me.

Chapter Three

The Wall

One day while I was working at PEA in Whitesboro, Texas, I was in a stall with an Intern from Italy named Isabella. I was restraining this enormous weaning halter horse filly-basically yearling-sized. The stalls in the hospital were 12x12 and made of metal framed concrete walls, roughly 4.5 feet tall with metal bars going up probably another 4.5 feet I guess. I would press young horses up against those walls with my body, brace myself with one hand on the bar, hook my other arm up under their jaw so their head rested over my elbow, and then reach up with that same hand to twist an ear. And 99.9% of the time, it worked to keep them perfectly still.

But this day that big filly went up and she managed to take me up in the air with her and when I came back down with her I cracked my right temple on the edge of the metal frame on the concrete so hard and the lights went off and on, off and on and I swear I saw tweety birds and heard bells ringing.

That's one of the hardest times I have ever hit my head in my whole life. I remember one of the guys working in the barn named Carlos coming up to me after it was all said and done saying "Amy you no more work here..you go work Walmart..Walmart safe for you!"

Chapter Four

Learning The Hard Way

When I was about 4, my family was visiting a friend's house and they had horses in their barn. I snuck off without any shoes to the barn to go see the baby horse that was in there. I went inside the old dairy barn with its concrete floor and walked over to the mare, and she let me pet her and the foal.

There were flies, I remember, and I learned my first lesson about being aware of where a horse was going to put its hoof when hers landed on my little barefoot between the concrete. I managed to push her off of me and limped away knowing I couldn't let anybody know I was hurt because I wasn't supposed to be out—the first of many of those times I had to suck it up so I didn't get in trouble for being with horses when I wasn't supposed to be. I learned quickly to pay attention — especially when hooves are involved.

The Black Stallion was my favorite movie. The story of Alexander the Great and Bucephalus was also my favorite story.

When I was about 5 or so, my aunt bought a 2 or 3-year-old black stallion from an auction and brought him to our house. I don't think he was even halter broke, and now he was living in our barn. They couldn't get the auction sticker off his butt for days. He got loose once, and as he was taking off through the yard, my dad caught him with his lariat—and he didn't let go of the rope when the horse took off down the road, dragging my dad behind him, ripping his arms to shreds.

Well, needless to say, I was not allowed to go near him, with or without an adult. So I used to sneak out at night, stealing sugar cubes from the kitchen on my way. I'd make my way out in the dark to the barn, and I would line sugar cubes on the top of his gate—three for him and one for me. I would sit on the top rail of his stall waiting for him to come to me, just so I could touch his soft muzzle.

One day, when I was 6, my mom must have been at work because she wasn't home, but my dad was taking a nap, so I took my opportunity to sneak out to see the horses. I don't know why I did it, but for some reason I always went through the gate—and I always seemed to leave it open. Two big horses got out along with one of my ponies, Princess, my jet black Shetland pony. I knew I was going to be in super big trouble if my dad got up and saw the horses out.

Somehow, I managed to get the big horses to go back into the pasture, but Princess got to the gate and would not budge. I pushed her, I pulled her, and I pushed her some more, and she just braced herself in refusal—stubborn pony.

There was a bushy tree, maybe a cedar, a few feet away, so I walked over, snapped a little twig off, and marched back stomping my feet. I stopped directly behind her, and let her have it with that switch right across her behind. She kicked me with both hooves and sent me flying backward, knocking the wind right out of me. I think I may have blacked out a little. Princess had now gone back to where she belonged, and I knew there was still the possibility of getting caught, so I made myself get up, got the gate shut and locked, and managed to make it to about the tree before I collapsed on the ground still trying to catch my breath.

Suddenly, lying on the ground, I saw my dad's shadow towering over me. "What happened, Aim?" he asked. I told him I'd been running and tripped over a rock, still barely able to breathe. I didn't confess what had really happened until years later. He just laughed and shook his head. I learned very early that when you hit the ground—you've got to get up again.

I used to sneak out into the pastures. I was happy watching them, always wishing I would turn into one. I learned how to read body language. Some of the time I would climb up while they were grazing and just lay back and stare at the clouds, back to back. And other times I was instigating a game of chase, and I would be running with the horses. It always felt like that's where I belonged.

When I was about 6 or 7 my cousin Terry came to spend the summer with us, she was around 16 or so. My parents may have been gone when she decided she was going to take Glory for a ride but she told me I couldn't go.

Needless to say this did not go over well with me.

I snuck out of the house and caught Princess. I put her hackamore on in the pen and proceeded to lead her towards the 200 acre field.

I could see them almost in the middle of the field of tall grass. Glory resting quietly with all her weight shifted onto one hip. Terry was laying back on Glory staring at the sky or looking at the back of her eyelids, I don't know, the reins rested on Glory's neck.

Princess and I snuck up behind them and neither of them seemed to notice.

As we approached them I grabbed my reins and I smacked Glory on the butt and off she went! I was so tickled to watch my cousin frantic and bouncing around!

However, Terry caught her balance, and Glory stopped, and that feeling of reprisal suddenly changed. They changed direction and started coming for us! My little pony ran us all over the field, trying to outsmart my cousin who was screaming, 'I'm gonna beat you!"

My mom used to tell people I was a horse until I was about 16. I had two ponies: Princess and a half-Shetland, half-Welsh black pony whose face was mostly gray. He was old—really, really old—but he didn't act old. He was a handful, my old Coco. I was not allowed to ride with a saddle unless I had an adult with me for a long time, so I rode bareback daily because I never had an adult to ride with me.

When I was 8, my dad decided he wanted to give me his mare he had raised from a foal. Glory must have been about 4 or 5 then—a pretty flea bitten gray mare, half Arabian and half Quarter Horse. I remember the day he gave her to me, and she was officially mine. I was riding her in a circle around him, and he kept telling me to lope her.

I could just tell she was thinking something and posturing like she was going to buck, and I told him that. He laughed at me and said "She's never bucked once!", and told me to dismount so he could show me. He got her going into a gallop, made half a circle around me, and then she was almost standing on her head, back legs straight up in the air, with my dad flying out of the saddle. He hit the dirt, and I hopped off the fence laughing at him as he got up, knocking the dust off. I caught Glory, climbed back on, and took off in a lope circling him!

I fell of Glory PLENTY. Several times running bareback full speed across an open pasture and a bird would appear and she would disappear from under me.

I won my first trophy with her at 8 in my very first show—we beat all the grownups in the egg-and-spoon class that day!

When I was 9, we were at a show, and because it had rained that morning, the arena was too wet for the halter and showmanship classes, so we did them in front of the arena in a patch of dry-ish land. I always took Glory in the classes last because she didn't like being between two strange horses.

One morning, there was a horse at the beginning of the lineup dancing around and acting up, so the judge asked them to move to the end. I had my back to the horse at this time and was watching the judge approach when suddenly I was struck in the back by that horse's hoof and lifted into the air, thrown into Glory's neck, causing her to stumble. I was stunned for a second. My shoulder blade was sore, but I was able to recover. I could see everyone staring with their eyes bulging and mouths open.

I got up, dusted myself off, and made sure Glory was okay. The grownups all sat back down, and we finished the class after the disruptive horse was excused. For many years I could feel a strange little moving chip on my shoulder blade from when it happened but it's been a long time since I could reach my arms back to check again!

Chapter Five

Magic

When I was 12 I had both of my ponies and my big girl Glory. I had been showing since I was 8 and I was having a lot of fun. I saw how girls would react when they didn't get the ribbon they thought they deserved. My mom always told me she appreciated that I didn't have tantrums if I didn't do well. They would take it out on their horse, and I always looked at it this way: I understood if I didn't place, but if I got 5th place out of 10 riders, I beat 5 riders and was happy with that.

By the time I was about 12 years old, I wanted to improve in the arena. Glory was amazing, but she was just Glory—not bred to the hilt, nor could my parents afford silver-laden halters, bridles, or saddles, let alone a horse trainer. I wanted to compete in the Western and English classes. Chasing barrels and weaving through poles was great fun and exciting, but to me, the pleasure classes were much more technical and challenging.

So when I was 12, I saved all my babysitting money and bought a pretty black weanling filly that I named Magic. Her sire was a buckskin Quarter horse named Cody and her dam was a hefty black thoroughbred and Morgan mare named Shay-tahn, though she was no Cass Ole.

I registered my filly with the half Quarter horse association. Magic was the first horse I fully trained. We were in the 4-H horse training project and won at county every time, and moved on to win at state also when she was 2 or 3, I think. She was very intelligent and willing, so we learned a lot together. She could gallop beautifully in place and pirouette like a pro before she was 4 and I developed a love for dressage with her.

I would often ride her bareback and bridle-less. I could just say the word left or right with no other cue simply the word and she would take off in that lead and then do a flying lead change with the next verbal cue only.

I received a beautiful dark oil, split ear silver show headstall for Christmas one year. And we were able to buy a used saddle with silver. I had watched the people that were winning and did what they were doing. Magic and I practiced every day—rain or shine, snow or sun. I knew if I wanted high point, I had to compete and place well in all the Western and English classes. At the time, I did not like English at all. I read so many books about English riding and dressage.

My idol was a woman who lived down the road from us named Cheryl P. She was about 8 years older than me and was the hardest working woman I had known. She worked 2 jobs, had around 20 horses, and her barn was always immaculate. She was always the one who would pull into a show and clean house. She used to haul me and some other girls around to shows with her.

I'll never forget the day she came to pick Magic and me up, and we went to a show where Cheryl and I were now in open Senior classes competing against each other.

We entered the first class, always halter. They announced the winner......it was me and Magic! Second class, showmanship, they announced the winner in first place—it was me!! All day, every class, I won first place! We took home every trophy that day!! We won high point for the first time, and it was so satisfying!!

Cheryl's mother had been there that day, and I heard her when she walked out to Cheryl and snarled, "Well, it would have been nice if you would have brought home at least one blue ribbon today."

I gleamed! I proudly loaded my little ragamuffin mare back on her trailer, and she hauled us home. I will never forget my dad meeting us in the drive to help unload all my gear, and as I started handing him trophy after trophy, the look on his face was priceless as he smiled when I told him they were all mine!! Hard work, persistence, and a little grit can turn any horse into a champion.

Magic and I had gotten a ride to one of the several Lloyd Anderson clinics put on in Proctor MN in the 90s with my idol Cheryl, along with another girl and her horse. Cheryl had this awesome, 4 horse slant load with the tack in the back and Magic loved to go places in that trailer. In between our lessons I had gone to swap saddles and my English saddle was sitting on the top saddle rack in the tack compartment.

We walked up to the trailer and both doors were barely cracked open. I swung the tack door open, took a step up onto the trailer to slide my arm completely under the saddle, and was beginning to lift it off the rack as Magic nudged the other door open with her nose and proceeded to let herself in. I tugged on her rope to gently pull her backwards, and I accidently leaned my back up against the door swinging it open as my bra strap went over a bridle rack hook as Magic backed up, opening the door completely!

There I was, dangling like a dummy from the inside of the trailer door, and Magic in one hand just lookin at me like 'what now?' while I held my English saddle over my other arm. I couldn't even reach the trailer with my legs!! A mom happened to be walking by and saw me hanging there and laughingly asked me if I needed any help!

I had so much fun with Magic, and she was capable of so much. I remember one cold winter day, I was 16 or 17, and I had just finished working Magic. I put her in her stall, gave her grain, and was turning to go out the door when my younger sister Kym started yelling that our younger sister Keri Ane was attempting to run away. You should know, Keri Ane was the bookworm in the family and never spent much time outdoors. All of this was happening as a blizzard was beginning to set in, and our parents were not home.

So I went to my 1978 F150, 3-on-the-tree, bucket of rust, and it wouldn't start. My next means of transportation was in her stall, happily doing her favorite thing—eating her grain. I took a piece of twine hanging near her stall, wrapped it around her neck, and insisted we leave her stall and food to go out into a blizzard and down the road. She was not having it.

I climbed on her bareback, with just the twine wrapped around her neck, and proceeded to convince her to follow my sister. She bucked and crow-hopped much of the way as I followed Keri Ane, who had now made it about three-quarters of a mile down a dirt road.

Once we caught up to my sister, I blocked her from going any further and informed her she was in a blizzard. She looked at me and said, "Give me a ride back!"

No way!! She didn't see what I rode with a piece of twine to get to her! I told her it was her own fault she was out there in the first place and made her walk back while I rode the bronco in the blizzard!

Chapter Six

The Racetrack

Glory had been off our property very few times when we attended the county fair for the first time. I lived for the county fair. The smells of fried foods, the sound of all the carnival rides and games going on, so many barns filled with wonderful things to look at. From home grown giant vegetables and arts and crafts to wandering through the livestock barns filled with cows, pigs and chickens and the petting areas with rabbits and goats galore.

But my favorite of course was always the horse barn. The smell of all the horses, the leather, all the different flysprays and show sheens. Horses in the stalls covered in sheets and tails braided and hung in bags. Signs of different shapes, sizes and materials hanging from the stalls identifying horse and young rider. My mom was very talented and she painted many of the signs hanging in the barn including my own with Alerts Glory painted in black letters outlined in silver if I remember correctly.

Every year the fair was kicked off with a grand entry COSTUME parade around the horse racetrack, so all entries were in costume. My auntie Gale was a remarkable seamstress who had had her own shop making costumes in Southern California and she had given us several. I found a native American costume, I don't remember what it was made of but it looked like I was wearing long sleeve buckskin with fringe and all. At 8 years old or so I had my hair braided and I may have been barefoot also. There was this 2" elastic belt covered in turquoise sequins. It had long leather strings with a couple of white feathers hanging off of the belt with two big white feathers.

Now...I was riding her bareback sitting on a Navajo blanket, she was a slick and squeaky clean horse and a Navajo blanket equaled nothing but slipping and sliding with every step! As we all started to gather around and make our way to the racetrack there were other horses dressed up in bigger more elaborate costumes, we had our photo taken next to a girl wearing a huge southern belle dress and her horse had a big bonnet and Glory would not, could not stand still.

She saw a cow for the first time, and that cow was also wearing a costume of some sort, by this time I was focused only on staying on. To make matters worse as we were entering the entrance of the racetrack my mom decided that Glory should wear the belt around her neck! So she stretched the belt over her head, and around Glory's neck and suddenly as the wind blew the feathers she saw it fly with the corner of her eye and weeeee my horse was sliding out from underneath me a hundred miles an hour in every direction at once and it took everything I had to maintain my balance and stay on her back! Either my mom or dad was able to get the belt off her but it was too late, she was so overwhelmed I couldn't calm her, and there was no way she was going to just walk like everyone else.

So she and I rode sideways, forward and backwards, terrified at any second I was going to just slide right off of her! The hardest part was going in front of the grandstand with the bleachers packed full of people hooting and hollering, stomping their feet and clapping their hands, kids running back and forth along the rail with the procession of tractors and animals in costumes trailing behind us. Somehow I rode her dancing and spinning, crow hopping and trying to take off all the way around the track.

I have often wondered back to this memory and wondered what my parents were thinking!!

Chapter Seven

The Pregnant Rodeo

When I was little as I've said, I fell off plenty and I got bucked off plenty. But there came an age that I learned how to tell that a buck was coming and how to altogether prevent a horse from bucking in the first place. I don't think I got bucked off or fell off a horse from about age 11 or 12.

I was almost 22 and I had been discharged from the Army in Ft. Lewis, Washington, where I served almost 3 years as a diesel mechanic. I had started training horses again while my "fiancé/ex-husband" was finishing his enlistment. I had been riding and showing this 17-some-hand gelding for a woman in some English classes. She knew I was about 5 months pregnant at the time and I remember her coming into the arena one day I was riding her horse bareback and she started crying because she was worried I was going to fall.

Her horse and I had been doing really well together and one day she asked me if I'd be willing to go to her house where she had a younger mare that had some 60 days of professional training 6 months prior to being turned out to pasture. Of course I agreed! When I got to her house that day, she had told me that she had aced (mild sedation) the mare. I remember thinking "why would you do that if you have a trainer coming out?", but I just shrugged it off. I myself had never had a need to use it for anything besides cleaning sheaths, so at that time I was unaware that it could have adverse effects.

I did my normal routine when dealing with a new horse. I liked to lunge them a bit to get to know them and for them to get to know me. I did this for a while and once I was comfortable with where I thought she was, I approached her, bridled her, and I proceeded to mount her. She stood perfectly still for me. That was until my right leg came down her side — and she exploded like a bronc coming out of the chutes. I didn't last a second! I hit the ground tucking and rolling, making sure I landed on my back! The lady instantly burst into tears asking me if I was okay.

I got up, dusted off and said, "Yup… let's try that again."

Again I came right down! Now the lady is pleading with me to stop, but I couldn't! You fall off, you get back on! I was mad that I fell off — I didn't get bucked off horses! I was so determined to ride this horse! I ended up taking the saddle off so I could just slide off and not get hung up on anything.

She bucked me off again!! Five times I came off that mare and I kept getting madder and madder. For the first time in my life I had to let the horse win — I was, after all, 5 months pregnant and my life wasn't the only one at stake so fully frustrated and a bit beat up I had to call it quits.

I used to joke and say that getting bucked off her split my one baby into 2 because little did I know I was actually carrying twins!! And I would get bucked off plenty more later in life!

Chapter Eight

The Cloned Stallion

At about 25, I was working as a vendor at Lowe's in Sherman, Texas. One day, I saw an ad in a paper for a veterinary technician at an all-equine clinic in Whitesboro, Texas. I didn't think I'd get it, but I did!

I was hired as a floating technician, helping where extra hands were needed and doing tasks others didn't want, including assisting euthanasia and necropsies.

One day, I was asked to hold a stallion in the stocks to scope him for strangles. He had been sedated and had a twitch on his nose. Everything was calm and quiet, until it wasn't. The stallion reared up, and his upper body flipped over the top of the side rail! I pulled as hard as I could to get him back inside the stocks. Dr. Rhoads and the trainer just stared at me, mouths open! Dr. Rhoads exclaimed, "Do you realize you just saved his life?"

 I did not, I just thought I did what anybody would do.

Well I climbed the ladder quickly and was promoted to Dr. Rhoads' 2nd technician. I helped do lameness exams, surgeries, emergencies — you name it.

My schedule allowed me to work around my kids' schedule so I came in early and I helped the interns do all the morning stuff: TPR every horse in the clinic, draw blood, give meds, flush catheters, hang fluids and plasma, etc. Horses were kept in the lameness area, in the hospital, in the ICU and in quarantine. We had several quarantine areas at that time because we also conducted bone scans and horses needed to be injected with a radioactive isotope, and that required quarantine.

This was an enormous and prestigious operation and I LOVED IT. We were only one part of the facility located in several barns. The other half of the clinic was the reproduction side. Dr. Hartman is a legend in the field. We housed legendary stallions and because of the caliber clients we had, we also maintained a herd of about 3000 recipient mares used as surrogate mothers — incubators basically. Many of them were once bound for slaughterhouses and saved because they had a womb. Essentially, they are wild horses or become that way because their sole purpose in life is to carry another mare's baby and they don't get handled enough.

Some of those babies were clones! Seven of nine Smart Chic Olena clones, all a variety of sorrels like their donor but none of them looked alike nor did they look like him. They were supposed to go overseas, but they ended up staying on the clinic property for a couple of years. There was a single Doc's Serendipity cloned filly, who embodied what you expect a clone to look like. And one year we had 3 clones that came from a famous polo stallion - that was one of my muddiest foal rescues ever!

Chapter Nine

The Mule

After I had been working with Dr. Rhoads and his tech for about 2 years and there was no room for me to advance. There were other girls that had been working there long before me that were still just floating technicians hoping to move up. So when I went to Dr. Easter, asking to be a floating tech again, he made me a laboratory technician. He also made me responsible for purchasing EVERYTHING in the facility — every supply, every drug — and when Dr. Easter wanted me, he told me he wanted me to be right there, so under no circumstances was I to leave my post. I still helped the interns in the morning, but once rounds were done I was in the lab running tests, sending things off, and handling the orders.

One day all of the techs, seven at least, along with Dr. Easter, were all inside the lab. I remember the reception area was full when I looked out my lab window near the door where Dr. Easter stood when Dr. Kate came in from the exam room and said "Amy and Amy alone come with me!"

I looked at Dr. Easter and he said nothing so I went with her.

We walked out the exam room and through the hospital to a dark gray slant load goose neck trailer backed into the hospital barn door.

As we opened the trailer door, we could see he had actually got locked in the partition closest to the gooseneck, only he was facing backwards! To my complete surprise, he hadn't yet attempted to jump out the side window yet!

We got on the trailer and we approached him slowly, and I could see when he was thinking, and I was able to redirect his thinking with my hand, very slowly and gently, steering him away from the window but also away from the doctor at the same time so she could quickly inject him. She was able to inject the sedation into the big bulging vein in his neck and he didn't move, eyes fixed on my hand.

Just like that, we opened his partition and I was able to carefully help him lay down.

Once he laid down, she gave the word for the barn guys to come help drag him off the trailer onto the gurney on wheels and into surgery, where Dr. Kate sutured his injury. As he was in recovery, I was tasked with his handling and in-house training so he would be able to be doctored in the future.

On another day, as we were cleaning the surgery room Dr. Rhoads had come in and said "Amy and Amy alone come with me."

And on the way from the hospital barn to the breeding barn I was told not to breathe a word about what I was going to see.

Inside the building standing in the stocks I saw a yearling with some sores on his hide caused by a very rare disease called HERDA from a very distinguished ranch. Something I never expected to see, hereditary equine regional dermal asthenia.

Chapter Ten

Legends In Person

During my time at P.E.A. I had gotten a tour of a very special ranch. I remember walking into Carol Rose's trophy room and seeing the vast shelving from floor to ceiling around every corner of this huge room. The shelves were lined all the way from top to bottom with AQHA world champion trophies, and there was this amazing, gorgeous Charro saddle on display with a garland of roses draped over its enormous silver horn.

But nothing was more jaw-dropping than the sight of Zan Parr Bar's bronze shoes hanging on a plaque right there on the wall. I will never forget that.

Peptoboonsmal was there that day, and I let him lick my hand and arm. Shining Spark was there as well as expected, but almost as impressive as it was to see Zan Parr Bar's bronze shoes was seeing Genuine Doc grazing in a pen near the driveway!

Chapter Eleven

First Profession

Between my junior and senior year of high school I took a job working at a horse ranch near McGregor, Minnesota. I lived on this amazing property with amazing views, a big pole barn filled with stalls, a small indoor arena, a huge outdoor arena, and a REAL round pen!

Paradise for a horse crazy teenage girl! I don't remember the exact number of horses, but it was more than enough to keep me busy every day. Lots of foals to halter break, a few yearlings to work with, and a 2-year-old or two to break. They had plenty of mature and broke horses, and a few of them I would show.

They had a beautiful Dunn Quarter Horse stallion named Lem. I'll never forget the scenes I saw there. I remember the guy taking Lem out of the barn one morning when the sun was coming up, and all I could see as they walked out were their silhouettes as Lem reared straight up. It was beautiful to see.

As it would be at sunset when the mares and foals would charge back to the barn when I would call them, I could hear the thunder of so many hooves and all I could see were the dark silhouettes against the sunsets.

I lived there for the summer with my big Paint gelding Mickey. My reward for working there those months was my choice of horse from a selection of about 8 or 9, in a variety of ages from weanling up to 2 and 3 year olds.

I picked a gorgeous solid bay 4 month old stud colt named Vaquero — he was beautiful.

When I was a senior in high school, I enlisted in the military. But I took the summer off before going to basic training.

So I took a job as a horseback trail guide that spring, and I hauled the big paint Mickey and 1-year-old Vaquero to the Minnesota and Canadian border, where Mickey and I would guide groups of riders on rented horses through the Gunflint Trail.

I used to have to get up early every morning to track down horses because the moose would just walk right through the fences. In all my life, I have never even laid my eyes on a moose!

Chapter Twelve

The Wise Horse

When I was 9 I decided I wanted to leave home… no real reason other than I just felt like it was time for me to be on my own. I woke up real early one morning — must have been September or October — and I snuck out of the house taking nothing, but I did leave a note saying I was gonna be alright and maybe come back one day for my birthday presents or something. My only plan was taking my horse Glory and hitting the road.

I made it out to the pasture in the dark and was trying to catch my horse but she knew it was a stupid idea and wouldn't let me catch her. I did every trick I knew to try to catch her but I couldn't get close!

I turned at one point and saw the kitchen light come on, so I knew that meant my dad was getting up for work at 4 am, and it was do-or-die. So I stashed my halter and bridle, and I left my horse behind, and started down the road in the dark, middle of nowhere, Northern Minnesota.

We had a neighbor not far down the road, but beyond their property began the woodline. There the woods went on and on, and I didn't want to be in the woods in the dark. So I made it up the neighbor's drive and figured I'd hang out with their dog till the sun came up. Well, I had fallen asleep in the doghouse and woke to the sound of helicopters.

Curious what the helicopter was doing so low, I went outside to see it landing in my family's pasture! Driven by curiosity I started back towards home to see what was going on— only to be met by my grandfather on the road, who hugged me and asked me where I'd been!

Chapter Thirteen

The Horses And The Ponies

I had a lot of people trying to give me horses as a veterinary technician, and I always had too many already to take another. There have been occasions that I have taken in horses but for the most part I would have to say no.

I would have people call me and ask me to come and look at their horses' injuries all of the time, and I would always start off with, "I am not a vet."

And I would always encourage them to contact their veterinarian. A lot of the time they were calling me because they couldn't afford the vet. And most of the time when they would beg and I would cave and I would go do my best and insist they still contact a vet as I treated whatever the issue and they never would.

And on the rare occasion they would take my advice and have the vet out they wouldn't follow the doctors instructions either. Melting corneas to dummy foals and everything in between. That took a toll on me. It was hard to deal with being put in that situation.

There was a time after I had gotten divorced and moved back to MN and was staying with my parents. My mom got a phone call from a good friend of the family whom I'd known since his mare stepped on my little barefoot all those years ago. He had another mare with a four-month-old foal and had found her a week earlier with a bad cut on her back leg. He wasn't sure how bad it was, so he asked my mom if I would come take a look at it.

I insisted he have his vet look at it and make the diagnosis. Well, he called more than one day in a row, and my mom gave me the "he's a friend of the family," speech and she was right—he was—so I went to his house.

As I drove all the way out to his farm and up to his house, I could see his pasture, full of piles of rocks and rusty tid bits of old equipment. It's a wonder any of his horses and the neighbors' horses even had any legs walking through there. We walked to a section of his pasture where the mare and her foal were grazing.

She had a laceration visible about four inches or so above her right rear pastern, and then when she went to take a step, her leg went up but the hoof remained flat for a moment, as she had severed her leg to the bone!

I couldn't understand why he needed me to tell him this was bad. And after I went there, and after I told him the outcome probably wasn't good if he didn't have it treated—if it could be treated at this point. I found out days later she was finally put down.

One day while working at the vet clinic in Whitesboro, Tx. I got a phone call from a girl I barely knew and hadn't recently spoken to.
She called and asked if I'd go out to her sister's place to look at a yearling filly that had a laceration. I said no and gave my typical "call the vet" speech. She kept going on and pleading with me, and I finally caved.

After about an hour's drive, I arrived and was taken into the backyard. Outside, tied to a tree, was the grossest ragged little yearling I had ever seen. She was short and stunted with these ears that were too long for her head, a big wormy belly, and a nasty long dull red coat. Dirty.

On top of being unattractive, she had a terrible laceration on her left hind leg. Across the front of her pastern, from the inside to the outside, all the tendons and ligaments had been severed and were dangling out, covered in flies. It was bad.

I don't know how long the horses had been on the property. The sister's husband was a truck driver, and traveling through Florida he had seen a ranch with horses on his way home and on a whim decided to stop and buy some horses. He purchased the two yearlings and brought them to Texas.

The girl and I had convinced the sister to let us take the horse to the clinic to have it examined.

Dr. Rhoads told the owners she needed bandage changes every day for six months, or they could anesthetize her, suture it, and put a cast on to immobilize her pastern, which should heal with no scar. As nobody had any money, they asked me if I wanted her, and I said no thank you—I had enough horses as it was.

Well, she stayed in the clinic for a day or so, bandaged. The owners called me a few times asking if I wanted her, and I said no. Finally, they called again, and they would either like me to take her or they would bring her back and were going to "put a bullet in her!"

They had told me she was papered, and that I could have them, so I figured if nothing else, maybe I could use her as a broodmare when she was old enough. So I agreed to take her. I was given her papers, and I let Dr. Rhoads put the cast on.

She healed beautifully, as he said—no scar! By summer, she was turning into a yearling. My ugly duckling had turned into the most beautiful swan. She was absolutely stunning—so refined and defined, the most beautiful copper color with her flaxen blonde mane and tail. She had a pair of rear socks, a star, a stripe, and a snip. She grew into her ears and she was perfect!

She was the easiest horse I ever broke and the easiest to train. She had a very rare demeanor, and she never walked out of an area without a blue ribbon.

Aside from working at PEA in Whitesboro, TX, I went to work with Dr. S., who had a practice there and was opening a new satellite clinic not far from where my ex-husband and I had built our house, and I got hired to help her open it.

She was great and had great doctors that worked for her. It was an adjustment for me to work with her in the beginning after coming from so many years at PEA. There, everything was sterile and done in clean environments. Now, we were dropping a horse in the mud, removing an eyeball and checking the Farmer's Almanac to make sure the signs were right to castrate donkeys. And if the signs weren't right she wouldn't do it.

I remember working with Dr. S. one day at the satellite clinic. An ordinary stock trailer came rolling in with two horses on it and a frantic owner jumping out of the truck because one of her horses had been shot in the hip. She was so upset, crying and going on about her poor baby—her poor baby that was 2 or 3 years old and barely halter-broke, traveling with a buddy. We were trying to get some information about what had happened, and she kept putting her arm into the trailer, bawling and upsetting the horses. We had to ask her to step away from the trailer to continue to gather the information we needed. When we asked how long ago it had happened, she responded, "6 mo the ago!"

The doctors she had hired had also done their internships at PEA while I was a technician there, and because of that, they let me practice some advanced procedures that technicians don't usually get to do. I learned hands-on skills that gave me confidence and experience far beyond what I had done before, skills that would help me in the future.

After my divorce, I moved back to MN and I went to work for Dr. F. and Dr. K. at their mixed practice — dogs, cats, horses, and cows mostly. I remember Dr. F. pulling foals for us when I was a little kid and I mostly did cattle work with him while my sister (who did not like horses at all because they can be unpredictable and dangerous) would be drug along to do horse calls with his daughter Dr. K.

At the time I had taken a sabbatical from horses for a year or two after my divorce. I had so many people pulling on me to take care of horses, and they didn't want to treat the horses, and it all just stressed me out so bad I couldn't deal with them for a while. So I was content to just work with cows; cow owners are a lot easier to deal with.

I was asked to go one day with Dr. K., however and when we arrived at this property, she had picked out a little spotted foundered pony she wanted for one of her kids. The lady sold her the foundered pony, and then she asked me if I would want to just take this other pony she had in her herd.

Willow was dun with a long thick mane and tail just under 14hh. She had a pretty little face with a sweet blaze and a pair of socks. I was told she wasn't good for kids or adults and that's why I could just have her as she was rearing up with both. I didn't think about it too long before I agreed, thinking I'd figure out her issue and sell her.

But after the first time I rode her I loved her too much to sell her. So I added her to my herd, and she gave many riding lessons and put many smiles on little faces as well as mine.

One sub zero morning, I was woken by a frantic voice claiming there had been a commotion with the horses and she had been injured. I got out of bed and put my clothes on as quickly as I could, and as I went running out into the frigid air and falling snowflakes, I could see Willow being chased around the corral by a big sorrel gelding. I had just quit working at the vet clinic and had parted on bad terms (my whole family had a falling out with them), and the only other option was to haul her in bad weather for many hours south to a horse clinic in Southern MN.

The south side of my barn was open-faced. I had two stalls in the barn, a heated water tank for the horses, and then the horses had an area to come in from the weather also. The rest of the barn was filled with hay. It was minus 20 or 30 below zero that snowy day.

Here, Willow had a gash from mid-pectoral all the way around almost to her elbow — a clean cut, flesh and muscle flapping around. She was drenched in sweat, covered in snow and blood. What was I going to do?

My neighbor happened to have also worked with me at the clinic, and between people I knew I had all the necessary supplies to do what I didn't want to.

Someone had antibiotics from something, another person had suture and a skin stapler, I had extra sedation from something else. So we set up in one of my stalls. I sedated Willow and went to work, praying I was helping.

It was so cold. After the third pair of latex gloves broke because of the sub zero temperature — they literally just froze and broke into pieces — I just gave up wearing them. The suture kept snapping like it was made of glass, the stainless steel instruments were literally freezing to my hands because they were getting covered in blood.

I did the best I could, suturing the muscle and then closing the skin with the stapler, and everything looked great. But she wasn't out of the woods. I worried she would get an infection or that she would founder, so for days and nights I watched and worried.

She did great. I think the arctic cold contributed to her healing. About a week later, my neighbor came riding her horses over, and Willow stood in her stall looking out the open side, excited to see the other horse coming. She reared and bucked and carried on until she ripped the point of her chest open just a bit. But after it was all said and done, she didn't even have a scar — minus the dip in the point of her chest where she ripped out her sutures.

When I was in my mid 30s my dad had given my number to a co-worker and his wife. They had gotten a bargain on horses. Three horses for the price of one. One old broke mare (that hadn't been ridden in forever) and her 4 year old daughter and a gelding that were both barely halter broke. The people had no horse experience. I was very reluctant to help as they lived very far away and I had enough going on.

She offered to pay me handsomely so I agreed on the phone to meet with her the next day. I told her as we hung up that I would call her in the morning for directions and we would secure our time then.

When I called the next morning, she was very frantic. She told me that once she had hung up with me the night before, she had decided to saddle the broke mare. But once she got saddled, she received a phone call saying her daughter, who had been at a friend's house riding horses, had an accident.

So she told me that she was understandably in such a panic over her daughter that she left the horse with the saddle on, free in the pasture- which was also heavily forested-with two other horses overnight.

Thankfully, her daughter was ok but the owner had not gotten back from the ER until after midnight and decided it was too late to go out and take the saddle off. So now she can not catch the horse who still wore the saddle. I left immediately and drove as fast as I could. I parked in the driveway between the field and her house, where I could see her chasing the mare. The other horses weren't helping, running and carrying on. She saw me and we waved hello.

There was a dog barking at me and my truck and the owner exited the field to get her dog put away. I got out of my truck, and we passed each other along the way. The horses were still running around, and I could see the whole saddle had slid back so far from her withers it was half way down her back, and the girth was so tight it was digging in painfully.

I made it into the field and was able to immediately catch the mare, and before the owner had the dog in the house the saddle was on the ground.

The cinch was digging in so tight I had never had to pull so hard to get it loose. I could tell by the mare's movement just how painful it was, and she instantly stood still as soon as it fell off!

After I got the saddle off and the owner made her way back she was flabbergasted when she asked "How did you do that?"

I was upset with her for leaving the horse in a dangerous situation like that for that amount of time. After I got done telling her what I thought about what she had done and how lucky she was, she still wanted my help. She offered to pay me more. She convinced me she was determined to keep them and truly wanted to learn so I agreed and I helped her a couple times a week for a couple months.

Long ago my dad had done an apprenticeship when I was a kid with our farrier, a great horseman named Steve S. I remember my dad got kicked in the knee and later hurt his back, and he just couldn't do it anymore—but he still picked up his tools occasionally and did some work on our horses until his back gave out.

One day in my mid 30s he told me that if I did an apprenticeship with Steve also, he would give me all of his tools. So I called Steve up and started going out with him every chance I got. I learned a lot from him.

Even with all the knowledge and experience I had gained from working as a veterinary technician and doing an apprenticeship, I decided to take it one step further and took a two-week horseshoeing course at Heartland Horseshoeing School in Missouri.

I had been around people most of my career who expected you to make a horse stand still whatever way you had to, and I found instead I had to learn how to work with the horse to make them as comfortable as possible—most of the time making myself uncomfortable to make them comfortable. Some horses for example don't want their legs up high, flexing their knees, and they resist. It usually turns into a fight between a farrier and horse. But my back and body could take being in awkward positions, and I could read the horse. I got very popular for being able to trim horses other farriers weren't able to trim. And I without a fight—usually with just me and the horse, holding the horse and trimming at the same time. Horses that had reared up and fought every foot with every farrier gave me no trouble.

But one day, I went to a woman's house in Wisconsin. I had done a horse or two, then I caught the next horse that I had done before. I led the Anglo Arabian gelding out of the pasture, and tied him up to a hitching post.

By this time in my life when I had a horse behind me I knew exactly what they were doing -what ear was twitching, what hoof they were picking up and if they were being naughty. And if I had contact with a horse, I could feel everything before it happened. If a leg was going to move, I knew about it. This horse never twitched.

I bent over to pick up the front left leg. KABLAM! I got struck in the face!

The lights were going on and off, and I was trying to keep them on while moving away from the horse. The woman was screaming, "Are you okay!? Oh my God, are you okay?"

My hand pressed against my jaw, trying to hold my face together because I was afraid it was going to fall off if I let go, so I didn't want to respond.

I made it to my truck and figured I better do the cigarette test—if I could smoke a cigarette, I'd survive. I looked in the mirror and had a huge goose egg under my left eye—it HURT.

I suspect a bee may have been involved, but the one lesson I've learned in life is this: Shit happens to the best of the best.

I smoked my Marlboro Red and the woman asked what I wanted to do. I said, "Finish trimming this horse!"

I had hoped to do another—but my eye had swollen too badly. So I packed it up and headed home—but not before stopping at the closest tavern, where I slammed four shots of Patron before heading home.

I showed up at my parents house the next day black eye and super swollen cheek. My mom met me on the front porch, saying, "I just don't know what I would have done if I had been there when it happened!"

Then she asked the silliest question she ever asked me. "Did you go to the doctor?"

I said, "No, what were they going to do, say, 'Gee, I bet that hurt'? It's not like you could put a cast on it…it seems to have healed just fine. It hurt to have the air touch my cheekbone just under my eye socket…for six months.

Another day in my 30s Dr. K. called me and asked me to come to her house to look at a horse she wanted to sell suddenly and quickly. She knew I was looking for a horse for my boyfriend at the time. His only experience with horses was stealing a ride on someone else's race horses when he was supposed to be cleaning their barn, brave but stupid. He wanted a horse very badly, and he definitely wanted an Appaloosa.

Dr. K. had purchased Elvis The King for one of her cousins who was a beginner also. She had a house with property directly across the road from the veterinary clinic she and Dr. F. owned.

She had the sellers park the trailer in the clinic parking lot with their two-horse trailer, and her cousin went into the escape door to back her new horse off the trailer. She was unaware of the butt chain still behind him, and when he felt it he moved forward and I was told she panicked and had put her hands up, and he panicked and flew backward again this time he flipped completely over backwards onto the paved driveway.

He spent a week in her pasture before the two women decided they wanted to load him and another horse into a different trailer—just your standard four-horse/livestock trailer—and he wasn't having it. Dr. K. had her trailer parked by her yard this time, and when he refused to get on, let's just say she used excessive force. He finally had enough and jumped onto the trailer, and as soon as he had all four feet on, he flew backwards and for a second time in a week, he flipped completely over backwards, but this time he hit his head on a children's wooden jungle gym/swing set, scalping his forehead.

A couple days later we were walking up to the big 16 hh guy. He was missing all of the skin from just between his eyes up to his forelock- his whole forehead-and he had some other minor scrapes and injuries too. Flies were covering the huge wound.

She asked me if I wanted to buy him… I sighed. I took him for a test ride and he was great for me. Then I watched the boyfriend clutch onto him with wonder and love, and no idea what he was doing. I thought sure, the horse would heal, sure he could be fine for someone with some work, and sure I could teach someone at the same time. So with great hesitation I agreed to buy him.

Luckily we lived only a few miles away and were able to ride him home to add him to the herd.

Over the next few weeks, we doctored his injuries and we all spent a lot of time in class together. I poured all the knowledge of advanced horsemanship I could into a beginner course. I tried so hard to emphasize safety first, and so many times I would wonder how they were both still alive novice and rank horse.

The big orange appy with his snowy white butt, was covered in scars everywhere you looked especially on his face and this earned him the name Ojiishiingwe, it means Scarface in Ojibwe. We called him OJ for short and it fit him.

The weather wasn't great, but we worked with him as much as possible. It took some time before he would go near a trailer without panicking but slowly we gained his trust again.

Just six weeks later, a local cowboy race was to take place, and we just had to go. I took Sage, a really fun and cute red roan mare I had been training (she could buck so high!!), and that morning OJ was easy to load and seemed to handle the ride just fine. I was nervous and excited, not because of all the obstacles that they would have to do, but also because at the finish line of the course was a trailer that your horse had to load into!

He was riding in a halter and lead rope as I watched them fly through the obstacle course like a pair that had done it together 100 times before, and as I bit my nails watching them charge back across the big open pasture leaving the last obstacle, closing in on the trailer in a hurry! I don't think OJ had come to a complete stop as they pulled up and the man slid off his back, taking the saddle off in the same motion as the trailer door opened—and OJ LEAPT on!!

The Conclusion

I have many more memories and stories from over 30 years with horses—broken bones, lessons, and quiet moments—but I feel the ones I have shared in this book are the ones that truly stand out.

It's difficult to believe it's been nearly 10 years since I have been close enough to smell a horse.

Though I may not stand in a barn today, I still carry every lesson, every triumph, and every quiet moment with them in my memory.

And here we are now in 2026 and once again it is the Year of the Horse and I'm compelled to share some of my stories with others!

In Tribute To

Charlie
Cody
Willy
Chico 1
Chico 2
Sky
Shadda
Itasca
Toby
Jack
Duke
Kodiak
Partner
Ricky
Streak
Scarlet
Cookie
Clyde
Dozer
Gypsy
Gretta
Luna
L.B.
Bill
Chief
To all the horses…

www.ingramcontent.com/pod-product-compliance
Lightning Source LLC
Chambersburg PA
CBHW051407130726
47987CB00007B/2896